Constitution of the State of Indiana and Amendments

CONSTITUTION

OF THE

STATE * OF * INDIANA

AND

AMENDMENTS.

BY AUTHORITY.

CHARLES F. GRIFFIN,

Secretary of State

WM. B. BURFORD, PRINTER, LITHOGRAPHER AND BINDER.

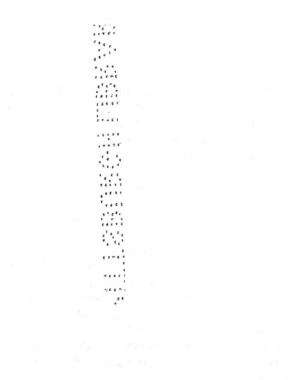

CONSTITUTION OF THE STATE OF INDIANA.

PREAMBLE.

To the end that justice be established, public order maintained, and liberty perpetuated: We, the people of the State of Indiana, grateful to Almighty God for the free exercise of the right to choose our own form of government, do ordain this Constitution.

ARTICLE I.

BILL OF RIGHTS.

SECTION 1. We declare that all men are created equal; that they are endowed by their Creator with certain unalienable rights; that among these are life, liberty, and the pursuit of happiness; that all power is inherent in the people; and that all free governments are, and of right ought to be, founded on their authority, and instituted for their peace, safety, and well being. For the advancement of these ends, the people have at all times an indefeasible right to alter and reform their government.

SEC. 2. All men shall be secured in their natural right to worship Almighty God according to the dictates of their own consciences.

SEC. 3. No law shall, in any case whatever, control the free exercise and enjoyment of religious opinions, or interfere with the rights of conscience.

SEC. 4. No preference shall be given, by law, to any creed, religious society or mode of worship; and no man shall be compelled to attend, erect or support any place of worship, or to maintain any ministry against his consent.

SEC. 5. No religious test shall be required as a qualification for any office of trust or profit.

SEC. 6. No money shall be drawn from the treasury for the benefit of any religious or theological institution.

SEC. 7. No person shall be rendered incompetent as a witness, in consequence of his opinion on matters of religion.

SEC. 8. The mode of administering an oath or affirmation shall be such as may be most consistent with, and binding upon, the conscience of the person to whom such oath or affirmation may be administered.

SEC. 9. No law shall be passed restraining the free interchange of thought and opinion, or restricting the right to speak, write, or print, freely, on any subject whatever; but for the abuse of that right every person shall be responsible.

SEC. 10. In all prosecutions for libel, the truth of the matters alleged to be libelous may be given in justification.

SEC. 11. The right of the people to be secure in their persons, houses, papers and effects, against unreasonable search or seizure shall not be violated, and no warrant shall issue, but upon probable cause, supported by oath or affirmation, and particularly describing the place to be searched, and the person or thing to be seized.

SEC. 12. All courts shall be open; and every man, for injury done to him, in his person, property or reputation, shall have remedy by due course of law. Justice shall be administered freely and without purchase; completely, and without denial; speedily, and without delay.

SEC. 13. In all criminal prosecutions the accused shall have the right to a public trial, by an impartial jury in the county in which the offense shall have been committed; to be heard by himself and counsel; to demand the nature and cause of the accusation against him, and to have a copy thereof; to meet the witnesses face to face, and to have compulsory process for obtaining witnesses in his favor.

SEC. 14. No person shall be put in jeopardy twice for the same offense No person, in any criminal prosecution, shall be compelled to testify against himself.

SEC. 15. No person arrested, or confined in jail, shall be treated with unnecessary rigor.

SEC. 16. Excessive bail shall not be required. Excessive fines shall not be imposed. Cruel and unusual punishment shall not be inflicted. All penalties shall be proportioned to the nature of the offense.

SEC. 17. Offenses, other than murder or treason, shall be bailable by sufficient sureties. Murder or treason shall not be bailable when the proof is evident, or the presumption strong.

SEC. 18. The penal code shall be founded on the principles of reformation, and not of vindictive justice.

SEC. 19. In all criminal cases whatever, the jury shall have the right to determine the law and the facts.

SEC. 20. In all civil cases the right of trial by jury shall remain inviolate.

SEC. 21. No man's particular services shall be demanded without just compensation. No man's property shall be taken by law without just compensation; nor, except in case of the State, without such compensation first assessed and tendered.

SEC. 22. The privilege of the debtor to enjoy the necessary comforts of life, shall be recognized by wholesome laws, exempting a reasonable amount of property from seizure or sale for the payment of any debt or liability hereafter contracted; and there shall be no imprisonment for debt, except in case of fraud.

SEC. 23. The General Assembly shall not grant to any citizen, or class of citizens, privileges or immunities which, upon the same terms, shall not equally belong to all citizens.

SEC. 24. No *ex post facto* law, or law impairing the obligation of contract, shall ever be passed.

SEC. 25. No law shall be passed, the taking effect of which shall be made to depend upon any authority, except as provided in this Constitution.

SEC. 26. The operation of the laws shall never be suspended except by the authority of the General Assembly.

SEC. 27. The privileges of the writ of *habeas corpus* shall not be suspended, except in case of rebellion or invasion, and then only if the public safety demand it.

SEC. 28. Treason against the State shall consist only in levying war against it, and giving aid and comfort to its enemies.

SEC. 29. No person shall be convicted of treason, except on the testimony of two witnesses to the same overt act, or upon his confession in open court.

SEC. 30. No conviction shall work corruption of blood or forfeiture of estate.

SEC. 31. No law shall restrain any of the inhabitants of the State from assembling together, in a peaceable manner, to consult for their common good ; nor from instructing their representatives; nor from applying to the General Assembly for redress of grievances

SEC. 32. The people shall have a right to bear arms for the defense of themselves and the State.

SEC. 33. The military shall be kept in strict subordination to the civil power.

SEC. 34 No soldier shall, in time of peace, be quartered in any house without the consent of the owner; nor in time of war but in a manner to be prescribed by law.

SEC 35 The General Assembly shall not grant any title of nobility, nor confer hereditary distinctions.

SEC. 36 Emigration from the State shall not be prohibited.

SEC 37 There shall be neither slavery nor involuntary servitude, within the State, otherwise than for the punishment of crime, whereof the party shall have been duly convicted. No indenture of any negro or mulatto, made or executed out of the bounds of the State, shall be valid within the State.

ARTICLE II.

SUFFRAGE AND ELECTION.

SECTION 1. All elections shall be free and equal.

SEC. 2. In all elections not otherwise provided for by this Constitution, every male citizen of the United States, of the age of twenty-one years and upwards, who shall have resided in the State during the six months, and in the township sixty days, and in the ward or precinct thirty days immediately preceding such election; and every male of foreign birth, of the age of twenty one years and upwards, who shall have resided in the United States one year, and shall have resided in this State during the six months, and in the township sixty days, and in the ward or precinct thirty days, immediately preceding such election, and shall have declared his intention to become a citizen of the United States, conformably to the laws of the United States on the subject of naturalization, shall be entitled to vote in the township or precinct where he may reside, if he shall have been duly registered according to law.

SEC. 3. No soldier, seaman or marine, in the army or navy of the United States, or their allies, shall be deemed to have acquired a residence in this State in consequence of having been stationed within the same; nor shall any such soldier, seaman or marine, have the right to vote

SEC. 4. No person shall be deemed to have lost his residence in the State by reason of his absence either on business of the State or of the United States

SEC. 5. [Stricken out by constitutional amendment of March 24, 1881.]

SEC. 6. Every person shall be disqualified from holding office during the term for which he may have been elected, who shall have given or offered a bribe, threat, or reward to procure his election.

SEC. 7. Every person who shall give or accept a challenge to fight a duel, or who shall knowingly carry to another person such challenge, or who shall agree to go out of the State to fight a duel, shall be ineligible to any office of trust or profit.

SEC. 8. The General Assembly shall have power to deprive of the right of suffrage, and to render ineligible any person convicted of an infamous crime.

SEC. 9. No person holding a lucrative office or appointment, under the United States, or under this State, shall be eligible to a seat in the General Assembly; nor shall any person hold more than one lucrative office at the same time, except as in this Constitution expressly permitted: *Provided*, That offices in the militia, to which there is attached no annual salary, and the office of Deputy Postmaster, where the compensation does not exceed ninety dollars per annum, shall not be deemed lucrative; *And provided, also,* That counties containing less than one thousand polls may confer the office of Clerk, Recorder and Auditor, or any two of said offices, upon the same person.

SEC. 10 No person who may hereafter be a collector or holder of public moneys, shall be eligible to any office of trust or profit until he shall have accounted for and paid over, according to law, all sums for which he may be liable.

SEC. 11. In all cases in which it is provided that an office shall not be filled by the same person more than a certain number of years continuously, an appointment *pro tempore* shall not be reckoned a part of that term.

SEC. 12. In all cases, except treason, felony and breach of the peace, electors shall be free from arrest in going to elections, during their attendance there, and in returning from the same.

SEC. 13 All elections by the people shall be by ballot; and all elections by the General Assembly, or by either branch thereof, shall be *via voce*.

SEC. 14. All general elections shall be held on the first Tuesday after the first Monday in November; but township elections may be held at such time as may be provided by law *Provided,* That the General Assembly may provide by law for the election of all judges of courts of general or appellate jurisdiction, by an election to be held for such officers only, at which time no other officer shall be voted for; and shall also provide for the registration of all persons entitled to vote.

ARTICLE III.

DISTRIBUTION OF POWERS.

SECTION 1. The powers of the Government are divided into three separate departments: the Legislative, the Executive (including the Administrative), and the Judicial; and no person charged with official duties under one of these departments shall exercise any of the functions of another except as in this Constitution expressly provided.

ARTICLE IV.

LEGISLATIVE.

SECTION 1. The Legislative authority of the State shall be vested in a General Assembly, which shall consist of a Senate and House of Representatives. The style of every law shall be, "Be it enacted by the General Assembly of the State of Indiana;" and no law shall be enacted except by bill.

SEC. 2. The Senate shall not exceed fifty, nor the House of Representatives one hundred members; and they shall be chosen by the electors of the respective counties or districts into which the State may, from time to time, be divided.

SEC. 3. Senators shall be elected for the term of four years, and Representatives for the term of two years, from the day next after their general election. *Provided, however,* That the Senators elect, at the second meeting of the General Assembly under this Constitution, shall be divided, by lot, into two equal classes, as nearly as may be; and the seats of Senators of the first class shall be vacated at the expiration of two years, and those of the second class at the expiration of four years; so that one-half, as nearly as possible, shall be chosen biennially forever thereafter. And in case of increase in the number of Senators, they shall be so annexed by lot, to the one or the other of the two classes, as to keep them as nearly equal as practicable.

SEC. 4. The General Assembly shall, at its second session after the adoption of this Constitution, and every sixth year thereafter, cause an enumeration to be made of all the male inhabitants over the age of twenty-one years.

SEC. 5. The number of Senators and Representatives shall, at the session next following each period of making such enumeration, be fixed by law, and apportioned among the several counties, according to the number of male inhabitants, above twenty-one years of age, in each: *Provided,* That the first and second elections of members of the General Assembly, under this Constitution, shall be according to the apportionment last made by the General Assembly before the adoption of this Constitution.

SEC. 6. A Senatorial or Representative district, where more than one county shall constitute a district, shall be composed of contiguous counties; and no county, for Senatorial apportionment, shall ever be divided.

SEC. 7. No person shall be a Senator or a Representative, who, at the time of his election, is not a citizen of the United States; nor any one who has not been, for two years next preceding his election, an inhabitant of this State, and for one year next preceding his election, an inhabitant of the county or district whence he may be chosen. Senators shall be at least twenty-five, and Representatives at least twenty one years of age.

SEC. 8. Senators and Representatives, in all cases except treason, felony, and breach of the peace, shall be privileged from arrest during the session of the General Assembly, and in going to and returning from the same; and shall not be subject to any civil process during the session of the General Assembly, nor during the fifteen days next before the commencement thereof. For any speech or debate in either House, a member shall not be questioned in any other place.

SEC. 9. The sessions of the General Assembly shall be held biennially, at the capital of the State, commencing on the Thursday next after the first Monday of January, in the year one thousand eight hundred and fifty-three, and on the same day of every second year thereafter, unless a different day or place shall have been appointed by law. But if, in the opinion of the Governor, the public welfare shall require it, he may, at any time, by proclamation, call a special session.

SEC. 10. Each House, when assembled, shall choose its own officers (the President of the Senate excepted), judge the elections, qualifications and returns of its own members, determine its rules of proceeding, and sit upon its own adjournment. But neither House shall, without the consent of the other, adjourn for more than three days, nor to any place other than that in which it may be sitting.

SEC. 11. Two-thirds of each House shall constitute a quorum to do business; but a smaller number may meet, adjourn from day to day, and compel the attendance of absent members. A quorum being in attendance, if either House fail to effect an organization within the first five days thereafter, the members of the House so failing shall be entitled to no compensation from the end of the said five days, until an organization shall have been effected.

Sec. 12. Each House shall keep a journal of its proceedings, and publish the same. The yeas and nays, on any question, shall, at the request of any two members, be entered, together with the names of the members demanding the same, on the journal: *Provided*, That on a motion to adjourn, it shall require one-tenth of the members present to order the yeas and nays.

Sec. 13. The doors of each House, and of Committees of the Whole, shall be kept open, except in such cases as, in the opinion of either House, may require secrecy.

Sec. 14. Either House may punish its members for disorderly behavior, and may, with the concurrence of two-thirds, expel a member; but not a second time for the same cause.

Sec. 15. Either House, during its session, may punish, by imprisonment, any person not a member, who shall have been guilty of disrespect to the House, by disorderly or contemptuous behavior in its presence; but such imprisonment shall not, at any time, exceed twenty-four hours.

Sec 16 Each House shall have all powers necessary for a branch of the legislative department of a free and independent State.

Sec. 17. Bills may originate in either House, but may be amended or rejected in the other, except that bills for raising revenue shall originate in the House of Representatives.

Sec. 18. Every bill shall be read by sections, on three several days in each House; unless. in case of emergency, two-thirds of the House where such bill may be depending shall, by a vote of yeas and nays, deem it expedient to dispense with this rule, but the reading of a bill by sections, on its final passage, shall in no case be dispensed with; and the vote on the passage of every bill or joint resolution shall be taken by yeas and nays.

Sec. 19. Every act shall embrace but one subject, and matters properly connected therewith; which subject shall be expressed in the title. But if any subject shall be embraced in an act, which shall not be expressed in the title, such act shall be void only as to so much thereof as shall not be expressed in the title.

SEC. 20. Every act and joint resolution shall be plainly worded, avoiding, as far as practicable, the use of technical terms.

SEC. 21. No act shall ever be revised or amended by mere reference to its title; but the act revised, or section amended, shall be set forth and published at full length.

SEC. 22. The General Assembly shall not pass local or special laws in any of the following enumerated cases, that is to say:

Regulating the jurisdiction and duties of justices of the peace and of constables;

For the punishment of crimes and misdemeanors;

Regulating the practice in courts of justice;

Providing for changing the venue in civil and criminal cases;

Granting divorces;

Changing the names of persons;

For laying out, opening and working on, highways, and for the election or appointment of supervisors,

Vacating roads, town plats, streets, alleys and public squares;

Summoning and impanneling grand and petit juries, and providing for their compensation;

Regulating county and township business,

Regulating the election of county and township officers, and their compensation,

For the assessment and collection of taxes for State, county, township or road purposes;

Providing for supporting common schools, and for the preservation of school funds;

In relation to fees or salaries; except that the laws may be so made as to grade the compensation of officers in proportion to the population and the necessary services required;

In relation to interest on money;

Providing for opening and conducting elections of State, county or township officers, and designating the places of voting;

Providing for the sale of real estate belonging to minors, or other persons laboring under legal disabilities, by executors, administrators, guardians or trustees

SEC. 23. In all the cases enumerated in the preceding section, and in all other cases where a general law can be made applicable, all laws shall be general and of uniform operation throughout the State.

SEC. 24. Provisions may be made by general law, for bringing suits against the State, as to all liabilities originating after the adoption of this Constitution; but no special act authorizing such suit to be brought, or making compensation to any person claiming damages against the State, shall ever be passed.

SEC. 25. A majority of all the members elected to each House shall be necessary to pass every bill or joint resolution; and all bills and joint resolutions so passed shall be signed by the presiding officers of the respective houses.

SEC. 26. Any member of either House shall have the right to protest, and to have his protest, with his reasons for dissent, entered on the journal.

SEC. 27. Every statute shall be a public law, unless otherwise declared in the statute itself.

SEC. 28. No act shall take effect until the same shall have been published and circulated in the several counties of this State, by authority, except in case of emergency; which emergency shall be declared in the preamble or in the body of the law.

SEC. 29. The members of the General Assembly shall receive for their services a compensation, to be fixed by law; but no increase of compensation shall take effect during the session at which such increase may be made. No session of the General Assembly, except the first under this Constitution, shall extend beyond the term of sixty-one days, nor any special session beyond the term of forty days.

SEC. 30. No Senator or Representative shall, during the term for which he may have been elected, be eligible to any office, the election to which is vested in the General Assembly, nor shall he be appointed to any civil office of profit, which shall have been created, or the emoluments of which shall have been increased, during such term; but this latter provision shall not be construed to apply to any office elective by the people.

ARTICLE V.

SECTION 1. The executive powers of the State shall be vested in a Governor. He shall hold his office during four years, and shall not be eligible more than four years in any period of eight years   .

SEC. 2. There shall be a Lieutenant Governor, who shall hold his office during four years.

SEC. 3. The Governor and Lieutenant Governor shall be elected at the times and places of choosing members of the General Assembly.

SEC. 4. In voting for Governor and Lieutenant Governor the electors shall designate for whom they vote as Governor, and for whom as Lieutenant Governor. The returns of every election for Governor and Lieutenant Governor shall be sealed up and transmitted to the seat of government, directed to the Speaker of the House of Representatives, who shall open and publish them in the presence of both Houses of the General Assembly.

SEC. 5. The persons, respectively, having the highest number of votes for Governor and Lieutenant Governor, shall be elected ; but in case two or more persons shall have an equal and the highest number of votes for either office, the General Assembly shall, by joint vote, forthwith proceed to elect one of the said persons Governor or Lieutenant Governor, as the case may be.

SEC. 6. Contested elections for Governor or Lieutenant Governor shall be determined by the General Assembly, in such manner as may be prescribed by law

SEC. 7. No person shall be eligible to the office of Governor or Lieutenant Governor, who shall not have been five years a citizen of the United States, and also a resident of the State of Indiana during the five years next preceding his election ; nor shall any person be eligible to either of the said offices who shall not have attained the age of thirty years.

SEC. 8. No member of Congress, or person holding any office under the United States, or under this State, shall fill the office of Governor or Lieutenant Governor.

SEC. 9 The official term of the Governor or Lieutenant Governor shall commence on the second Monday of January, in the year one thousand eight hundred and fifty-three; and on the same day every fourth year thereafter.

SEC. 10. In case of the removal of the Governor from office, or of his death, resignation or inability to discharge the duties of the office, the same shall devolve on the Lieutenant Governor; and the General Assembly shall, by law, provide for the case of removal from office, death, resignation, or inability, both of the Governor and Lieutenant Governor, declaring what officer then shall act as Governor; and such officer shall act accordingly until the disability be removed or a Governor be elected.

SEC. 11 Whenever the Lieutenant Governor shall act as Governor, or shall be unable to attend as President of the Senate, the Senate shall elect one of its own members as President for the occasion.

SEC. 12. The Governor shall be commander-in-chief of the military and naval forces, and may call out such forces to execute the laws, or to suppress insurrection, or to repel invasion.

SEC. 13 He shall, from time to time, give to the General Assembly information touching the condition of the State, and recommend such measures as he shall judge to be expedient.

SEC. 14 Every bill which shall have passed the General Assembly shall be presented to the Governor; if he approve, he shall sign it, but if not, he shall return it, with his objections, to the House in which it shall have originated, which House shall enter the objections at large upon its journals, and proceed to reconsider the bill. If, after such reconsideration, a majority of all the members elected to that House shall agree to pass the bill, it shall be sent, with the Governor's objections, to the other House, by which it shall likewise be reconsidered, and if approved by a majority of all the members elected to that House, it shall be a law. If any bill shall not be returned by the Governor within three days, Sundays excepted, after it shall have been presented to him, it shall be a law without his signature, unless the general adjournment shall prevent its return, in which case it shall be a law, unless the Governor, within five days next after such adjournment, shall file such bill, with his objections thereto, in the office of the Secretary of State, who shall lay the same before the General Assembly at its next session in like manner as if it had been returned by the Governor. But no bill shall be presented to the Governor within two days next previous to the final adjournment of the General Assembly.

SEC. 15. The Governor shall transact all necessary business with the officers of Government, and may require any information in writing from the officers of the administrative department, upon any subject relating to the duties of their respective offices.

SEC. 16. He shall take care that the laws be faithfully executed.

SEC. 17. He shall have the power to grant reprieves, commutations and pardons, after conviction, for all offenses except treason and cases of impeachment, subject to such regulations as may be provided by law. Upon conviction for treason, he shall have power to suspend the execution of the sentence until the case shall be reported to the General Assembly at its next meeting, when the General Assembly shall either grant a pardon, commute the sentence, direct the execution of the sentence, or grant a further reprieve. He shall have power to remit fines and forfeitures, under such regulations as may be prescribed by law, and shall report to the General Assembly at its next meeting, each case of reprieve, commutation or pardon granted, and also the names of all persons in whose favor remission of fines and forfeitures shall have been made, and the several amounts remitted: *Provided, however*, That the General Assembly, may, by law, constitute a council, to be composed of officers of State, without whose advice and consent the Governor shall not have power to grant pardons, in any case, except such as may, by law, be left to his sole power.

SEC. 18. When, during a recess of the General Assembly, a vacancy shall happen in any office, the appointment to which is vested in the General Assembly, or when, at any time, a vacancy shall have occurred in any other State office, or in the office of Judge of any court, the Governor shall fill such vacancy by appointment, which shall expire when a successor shall have been elected and qualified.

SEC. 19. He shall issue writs of election to fill such vacancies as may have occurred in the General Assembly.

SEC. 20. Should the seat of Government become dangerous from disease or a common enemy, he may convene the General Assembly at any other place.

SEC. 21. The Lieutenant Governor shall. by virtue of his office, be President of the Senate; have a right, when in Committee of the Whole, to join in debate, and to vote on all subjects, and, whenever the Senate shall be equally divided, he shall give the casting vote.

SEC. 22. The Governor shall, at stated times, receive for his services a compensation which shall neither bo increased nor diminished during the term for which he shall have been elected.

SEC. 23. The Lieutenant Governor, while he shall act as President of the Senate, shall receive for his services the same compensation as the Speaker of the House of Representatives; and any person acting as Governor shall receive the compensation attached to the office of Governor.

SEC. 24. Neither the Governor nor Lieutenant Governor shall be eligible to any other office during the term for which he shall have been elected.

ARTICLE VI.

ADMINISTRATIVE.

SECTION 1. There shall be elected by the voters of the State, a Secretary, an Auditor, and a Treasurer of State, who shall severally hold their offices for two years. They shall perform such duties as may be enjoined by law; and no person shall be eligible to either of said offices more than four years in any period of six years.

SEC. 2. There shall be elected in each county, by the voters thereof, at the time of holding general elections, a Clerk of the Circuit Court, Auditor, Recorder, Treasurer, Sheriff, Coroner, and Surveyor. The Clerk, Auditor and Recorder shall continue in office four years; and no person shall be eligible to the office of Clerk, Recorder or Auditor more than eight years in any period of twelve years. The Treasurer, Sheriff, Coroner, and Surveyor, shall continue in office two years; and no person shall be eligible to the office of Treasurer or Sheriff more than four years in any period of six years.

SEC. 3. Such other county and township officers as may be necessary, shall be elected or appointed, in such manner as may be prescribed by law.

SEC. 4. No person shall be elected or appointed as a county officer, who shall not be an elector of the county; nor any one who shall not have been an inhabitant thereof during one year next preceding his appointment, if the county shall have been so long organized; but if the county shall not have been so long organized, then within the limits of the county or counties out of which the same shall have been taken.

SEC. 5. The Governor, and the Secretary, Auditor and Treasurer of State, shall, severally, reside and keep the public records, books and papers, in any manner relating to the respective offices, at the seat of government.

SEC. 6 All county, township, and town officers shall reside within their respective counties, townships, and towns, and shall keep their respective offices at such places therein, and perform such duties as may be directed by law.

SEC. 7. All State officers shall, for crime, incapacity, or negligence, be liable to be removed from office, either by impeachment by the House of Representatives, to be tried by the Senate, or by a joint resolution of the General Assembly; two-thirds of the members elected to each branch voting, in either case, therefor.

SEC. 8. All State, county, township, and town officers may be impeached, or removed from office, in such manner as may be prescribed by law.

SEC. 9. Vacancies in county, township, and town offices shall be filled in such manner as may be prescribed by law.

SEC. 10. The General Assembly may confer upon the Boards doing county business in the several counties, powers of a local administrative character.

ARTICLE VII.

JUDICIAL.

SECTION 1. The Judicial power of the State shall be vested in a Supreme Court, in Circuit Courts, and in such other courts as the General Assembly may establish.

SEC. 2. The Supreme Court shall consist of not less than three, nor more than five Judges; a majority of whom shall form a quorum. They shall hold their offices for six years, if they so long behave well.

SEC. 3. The State shall be divided into as many districts as there are Judges of the Supreme Court, and such districts shall be formed of contiguous territory, as nearly equal in population as, without dividing a county, the same can be made. One of said Judges shall be elected from each district, and reside therein; but said Judge shall be elected by the electors of the State at large.

SEC. 4. The Supreme Court shall have jurisdiction, co-extensive with the limits of the State, in appeals and writs of error, under such regulations and restrictions as may be prescribed by law. It shall also have such original jurisdiction as the General Assembly may confer.

SEC. 5. The Supreme Court shall, upon the decision of every case, give a statement in writing of each question arising in the record of such case, and the decision of the Court thereon.

SEC. 6. The General Assembly shall provide by law, for the speedy publication of the decisions of the Supreme Court, made under this Constitution, but no judge shall be allowed to report such decision.

SEC. 7. There shall be elected by the voters of the State, a Clerk of the Supreme Court, who shall hold his office four years, and whose duties shall be prescribed by law.

SEC. 8. The Circuit Courts shall each consist of one judge, and shall have such civil and criminal jurisdiction as may be prescribed by law.

SEC. 9. The State shall, from time to time, be divided into judicial circuits, and a judge for each circuit shall be elected by the voters thereof. He shall reside within the circuit, and shall hold his office for the term of six years, if he so long behave well

SEC. 10. The General Assembly may provide, by law, that the judge of one circuit may hold the courts of another circuit, in cases of necessity or convenience; and in case of temporary inability of any judge, from sickness or other cause, to hold the courts in his circuit, provision may be made, by law, for holding such courts.

SEC. 11. There shall be elected, in each judicial circuit, by the voters thereof, a prosecuting attorney, who shall hold his office for two years.

SEC. 12. Any judge or prosecuting attorney, who shall have been convicted of corruption or other high crime, may, on information in the name of the State, be removed from office by the Supreme Court, or in such other manner as may be prescribed by law.

SEC. 13. The judges of the Supreme Court and Circuit Courts shall, at stated times, receive a compensation, which shall not be diminished during their continuance in office

SEC. 14 A competent number of justices of the peace shall be elected by the voters in each township in the several counties They shall continue in office four years, and their powers and duties shall be prescribed by law.

SEC. 15. All judicial officers shall be conservators of the peace in their respective jurisdictions

SEC. 16. No person elected to any judicial office shall, during the term for which he shall have been elected, be eligible to any office of trust or profit under the State, other than a judicial office.

SEC. 17. The General Assembly may modify or abolish the Grand Jury system.

SEC. 18. All criminal prosecutions shall be carried on in the name, and by the authority of the State; and the style of all processes shall be, "The State of Indiana."

Sec. 19. Tribunals of conciliation may be established, with such powers and duties as shall be prescribed by law; or the powers and duties of the same may be conferred upon other courts of justice; but such tribunals or other courts, when sitting as such, shall have no power to render judgment to be obligatory on the parties unless they voluntarily submit their matters of difference and agree to abide the judgment of such tribunal or court.

Sec. 20. The General Assembly, at its first session after the adoption of this Constitution, shall provide for the appointment of three commissioners whose duty it shall be to revise, simplify and abridge the rules, practice, pleadings and forms of the courts of justice. And they shall provide for abolishing the distinct forms of action at law now in use; and that justice shall be administered in a uniform mode of pleading, without distinction between law and equity. And the General Assembly may, also, make it the duty of said commissioners to reduce into a systematic code the general statute law of the State; and said commissioners shall report the result of their labors to the General Assembly, with such recommendations and suggestions, as to the abridgement and amendment, as to said commissioners may seem necessary or proper. Provision shall be made by law for filling vacancies, regulating the tenure of office and the compensation of said commissioners.

Sec. 21. Every person of good moral character, being a voter, shall be entitled to admission to practice law in all courts of justice.

ARTICLE VIII.

EDUCATION.

Section 1. Knowledge and learning generally diffused throughout a community, being essential to the preservation of a free government, it shall be the duty of the General Assembly to encourage, by all suitable means, moral, intellectual, scientific and agricultural improvement, and to provide by law for a general and uniform system of common schools, wherein tuition shall be without charge, and equally open to all.

SEC. 2   The common school fund shall consist of the congressional township fund, and the lands belonging thereto;

The surplus revenue fund;

The saline fund, and the lands belonging thereto;

The bank tax fund, and the fund arising from the one hundred and fourteenth section of the charter of the State Bank of Indiana;

The fund to be derived from the sale of county seminaries, and the moneys and property heretofore held for such seminaries; from the fines assessed for breaches of the penal laws of the State; and from all forfeitures which may accrue;

All lands and other estate which shall escheat to the State for want of heirs or kindred entitled to the inheritance;

All lands that have been or may hereafter be granted to the State, where no special purpose is expressed in the grant, and the proceeds of the sales thereof; including the proceeds of the sales of the Swamp Lands granted to the State of Indiana by the act of Congress, of the 28th of September, 1850, after deducting the expense of selecting and draining the same;

Taxes on the property of corporations that may be assessed by the General Assembly for Common School purposes.

SEC. 3.   The principal of the Common School Fund shall remain a perpetual fund, which may be increased, but shall never be diminished; and the income thereof shall be inviolably appropriated to the support of Common Schools, and to no other purpose whatever.

SEC. 4.   The General Assembly shall invest, in some safe and profitable manner, all such portions of the Common School Fund as have not heretofore been entrusted to the several counties; and shall make provisions, by law, for the distribution, among the several counties, of the interest thereof.

SEC. 5.   If any county shall fail to demand its proportion of such interest for Common School purposes, the same shall be reinvested for the benefit of such county.

SEC. 6.   The several counties shall be held liable for the preservation of so much of the said fund as may be entrusted to them, and for the payment of the annual interest thereon.

Sec. 7 All trust funds held by the State shall remain inviolate, and be faithfully and exclusively applied to the purposes for which the trust was created.

Sec. 8. The General Assembly shall provide for the election, by the voters of the State, of a State Superintendent of Public Instruction, who shall hold his office for two years, and whose duties and compensation shall be prescribed by law.

ARTICLE IX.

STATE INSTITUTIONS.

Section 1. It shall be the duty of the General Assembly to provide by law for the support of Institutions for the Education of the Deaf and Dumb, and of the Blind; and, also, for the treatment of the Insane.

Sec. 2. The General Assembly shall provide Houses of Refuge for the correction and reformation of juvenile offenders.

Sec. 3. The County Boards shall have power to provide farms as an asylum for those persons who, by reason of age, infirmity or other misfortune, have claims upon the sympathies and aid of society.

ARTICLE X.

FINANCE.

Section 1. The General Assembly shall provide, by law, for a uniform and equal rate of assessment and taxation; and shall prescribe such regulations as shall secure a just valuation for taxation of all property, both real and personal, excepting such only for municipal, educational, literary, scientific, religious or charitable purposes, as may be specially exempted by law.

Sec. 2. All the revenues derived from the sale of any of the public works belonging to the State, and from the net annual income thereof, and any surplus that may, at any time, remain in the Treasury derived from taxation for general State purposes, after the payment of the ordinary expenses of the government, and of the interest on bonds of the State, other than bank bonds, shall be annually applied, under the direction of the General Assembly, to the payment of the principal of the public debt.

SEC. 3. No money shall be drawn from the Treasury but in pursuance of appropriations made by law.

SEC. 4. An accurate statement of the receipts and expenditures of the public money shall be published with the laws of each regular session of the General Assembly.

SEC. 5. No law shall authorize any debt to be contracted, on behalf of the State, except in the following cases: To meet casual deficits in the revenue; to pay the interest on the State debt; to repel invasion, suppress insurrection, or, if hostilities be threatened, provide for public defense.

SEC. 6. No county shall subscribe for stock in any incorporated company, unless the same be paid for at the time of such subscription; nor shall any county loan its credit to any incorporated company, nor borrow money for the purpose of taking stock in any such company; nor shall the General Assembly ever, on behalf of the State, assume the debts of any county, city, town or township, nor of any corporation whatever.

SEC. 7. No law or resolution shall ever be passed by the General Assembly of the State of Indiana that shall recognize any liability of this State to pay or redeem any certificate of stock issued in pursuance of an act entitled "An act to provide for the funded debt of the State of Indiana, and for the completion of the Wabash and Erie Canal to Evansville," passed January 19, 1846, and an act supplemental to said act passed January 29, 1847, which by the provisions of the said acts, or either of them, shall be payable exclusively from the proceeds of the canal lands, and the tolls and revenues of the canal in said acts mentioned; and no such certificates of stocks shall ever be paid by this State.

[NOTE.—Agreed to by a majority of the members elected to each of the two houses of the General Assembly, Regular Session of 1871, and referred to the General Assembly to be chosen at the next general election Agreed to by a majority of the members elected to each house of the General Assembly, Special Session of 1872 Submitted to the electors of the State by an act approved January 28, 1873. Ratified by a majority of the electors, at an election held on the 18th day of February, 1873. Declared a part of the Constitution by proclamation of Thomas A. Hendricks, Governor, dated March 7, 1873.]

ARTICLE XI.

CORPORATIONS.

SECTION 1. The General Assembly shall not have power to establish, or incorporate any bank or banking company, or moneyed institution, for the purpose of issuing bills of credit, or bills payable to order or bearer, except under the conditions prescribed in this Constitution.

SEC. 2. No bank shall be established otherwise than under a general banking law, except as provided in the fourth section of this article.

SEC. 3. If the General Assembly shall enact a general banking law, such law shall provide for the registry and counter-signing, by an officer of State, of all paper credit designed to be circulated as money; and ample collateral security, readily convertible into specie, for the redemption of the same in gold or silver, shall be required; which collateral security shall be under the control of the proper officer or officers of the State.

SEC. 4. The General Assembly may also charter a bank with branches, without collateral security, as required in the preceding section.

SEC. 5. If the General Assembly shall establish a bank with branches, the branches shall be mutually responsible for each other's liabilities, upon all paper credit issued as money.

SEC. 6. The stockholders in every bank, or banking company, shall be individually responsible to an amount over and above their stock, equal to their respective shares of stock, for all debts or liabilities of said bank or banking company.

SEC. 7. All bills or notes issued as money, shall be, at all times, redeemable in gold or silver; and no law shall be passed, sanctioning, directly or indirectly, the suspension, by any bank or banking company, of specie payments.

SEC. 8. Holders of bank notes shall be entitled, in case of insolvency, to preference of payment over all other creditors.

SEC. 9. No bank shall receive, directly or indirectly, a greater rate of interest than shall be allowed by law to individuals loaning money.

Sec. 10. Every bank, or banking company, shall be required to cease all banking operations within twenty years from the time of its organization, and promptly thereafter to close its business

Sec. 11. The General Assembly is not prohibited from investing the trust funds in a bank with branches; but in case of such investment, the safety of the same shall be guaranteed by unquestionable security.

Sec 12. The State shall not be a stockholder in any bank, after the expiration of the present bank charter; nor shall the credit of the State ever be given, or loaned, in aid of any person, association, or corporation. nor shall the State hereafter become a stockholder in any corporation or association.

Sec. 13. Corporations, other than banking, shall not be created by special act, but may be formed under general laws.

Sec. 14. Dues from corporations, other than banking, shall be secured by such individual liability of the corporators, or other means, as may be prescribed by law.

ARTICLE XII.

MILITIA

Section 1. The militia shall consist of all able-bodied white male persons between the ages of eighteen and forty-five years, except such as may be exempted by the laws of the United States, or of this State; and shall be organized, officered, armed, equipped and trained in such manner as may be provided by law.

Sec 2. The Governor shall appoint the Adjutant, Quartermaster and Commissary Generals.

Sec. 3. All militia officers shall be commissioned by the Governor, and shall hold their offices not longer than six years.

Sec 4 The General Assembly shall determine the method of dividing the militia into divisions, brigades, regiments, battalions and companies, and fix the rank of all staff officers.

Sec. 5 The militia may be divided into classes of sedentary and active militia in such manner as shall be prescribed by law.

SEC. 6. No person conscientiously opposed to bearing arms shall be compelled to do militia duty: but such person shall pay an equivalent for exemption; the amount to be prescribed by law.

ARTICLE XIII.

POLITICAL AND MUNICIPAL CORPORATIONS.

SECTION 1. No political or municipal corporation in this State shall ever become indebted, in any manner or for any purpose, to any amount, in the aggregate exceeding two per centum on the value of taxable property within such corporation, to be ascertained by the last assessment for State and county taxes, previous to the incurring of such indebtedness, and all bonds or obligations, in excess of such amount, given by such corporations, shall be void: *Provided*, That in time of war, foreign invasion, or other great public calamity, on petition of a majority of the property owners, in number and value, within the limits of such corporation, the public authorities, in their discretion, may incur obligations necessary for the public protection and defense, to such an amount as may be requested in such petition.

[The original Article 13 is stricken out and the amendment of March 24, 1881, inserted in lieu thereof.]

ARTICLE XIV.

BOUNDARIES.

SECTION 1. In order that the boundaries of the State may be known and established, it is hereby ordained and declared, that the State of Indiana is bounded on the east by the meridian line which forms the western boundary of the State of Ohio; on the south by the Ohio River, from the mouth of the Great Miami River to the mouth of the Wabash River; on the west, by a line drawn along the middle of the Wabash River, from its mouth to a point where a due north line, drawn from the town of Vincennes, would last touch the northwestern shore of said Wabash River; and thence by a due north line, until the same shall intersect an east and west line, drawn through a point ten miles north of the southern extreme of

Lake Michigan; on the north, by said east and west line, until the same shall intersect the first-mentioned meridian line, which forms the western boundary of the State of Ohio.

SEC. 2.   The State of Indiana shall possess jurisdiction, and sovereignty co-extensive with the boundaries declared in the preceding section; and shall have concurrent jurisdiction, in civil and criminal cases, with the State of Kentucky on the Ohio River, and with the State of Illinois on the Wabash River, so far as said rivers form the common boundary between this State and said States respectively.

ARTICLE XV.

MISCELLANEOUS.

SECTION 1.   All officers whose appointment is not otherwise provided for in this Constitution, shall be chosen in such manner as now is, or hereafter may be, prescribed by law.

SEC. 2.   When the duration of any office is not provided for by this Constitution, it may be declared by law; and if not so declared, such office shall be held during the pleasure of the authority making the appointment.   But the General Assembly shall not create any office, the tenure of which shall be longer than four years.

SEC 3.   Whenever it is provided in this Constitution, or in any law which may be hereafter passed, that any officer, other than a member of the General Assembly, shall hold his office for any given term, the same shall be construed to mean that such officer shall hold his office for such term, and until his successor shall have been elected and qualified.

SEC. 4   Every person elected or appointed to any office under this Constitution shall, before entering on the duties thereof, take an oath or affirmation to support the Constitution of this State and of the United States, and also an oath of office.

SEC. 5.   There shall be a seal of the State, kept by the Governor for official purposes, which shall be called the Seal of the State of Indiana.

SEC. 6. All commissions shall issue in the name of the State, shall be signed by the Governor, sealed by the State Seal, and attested by the Secretary of State.

SEC. 7. No county shall be reduced to an area less than four hundred square miles; nor shall any county under that area be further reduced.

SEC. 8. No lottery shall be authorized, nor shall the sale of lottery tickets be allowed.

SEC. 9. The following grounds owned by the State in Indianapolis, namely: the State House Square, the Governor's Circle, and so much of out-lot numbered one hundred and forty-seven as lies north of the arm of the Central Canal, shall not be sold or leased.

SEC. 10. It shall be the duty of the General Assembly to provide for the permanent enclosure and preservation of the Tippecanoe Battle Ground.

ARTICLE XVI.

AMENDMENTS.

SECTION 1. Any amendment or amendments to this Constitution may be proposed in either branch of the General Assembly; and if the same shall be agreed to by a majority of the members elected to each of the two houses, such proposed amendment or amendments shall, with the yeas and nays thereon, be entered on their journals and referred to the General Assembly to be chosen at the next general election; and, if in the General Assembly so next chosen, such proposed amendment or amendments shall be agreed to by a majority of all the members elected to each house, then it shall be the duty of the General Assembly to submit such amendment or amendments to the electors of the State, and if a majority of said electors shall ratify the same, such amendment or amendments shall become a part of this Constitution.

SEC. 2. If two or more amendments shall be submitted at the same time, they shall be submitted in such manner that the electors shall vote for or against each of such amendments separately; and while such an amendment or amendments which shall have been agreed upon by one General Assembly shall be awaiting the action of the succeeding General Assembly, or of the electors, no additional amendment or amendments shall be proposed.

SCHEDULE.

This Constitution, if adopted, shall take effect on the first day of November, in the year one thousand eight hundred and fifty-one, and shall supersede the Constitution adopted in the year one thousand eight hundred and sixteen. That no inconvenience may arise from the change in the government, it is hereby ordained as follows.

First   All laws now in force, and not inconsistent with this Constitution, shall remain in force until they shall expire or be repealed.

Second.   All indictments, prosecutions, suits, pleas, plaints and other proceedings pending in any of the Courts, shall be prosecuted to final judgment and execution , and all appeals, writs of error, certiorari and injunctions shall be carried on in the several Courts, in the same manner as is now provided by law.

Third.   All fines penalties and forfeitures, due or accruing to the State, or to any county therein, shall inure to the State, or to such county in the manner prescribed by law   All bonds executed to the State, or to any officer, in his official capacity, shall remain in force, and inure to the use of those concerned.

Fourth.   All acts of incorporation for municipal purposes shall continue in force under this Constitution, until such time as the General Assembly shall, in its discretion, modify or repeal the same.

Fifth.   The Governor, at the expiration of the present official term, shall continue to act until his successor shall have been sworn into office.

Sixth.   There shall be a session of the General Assembly, commencing on the first Monday of December, in the year one thousand eight hundred and fifty-one.

Seventh. Senators now in office and holding over, under the existing Constitution, and such as may be elected at the next general election, and the Representatives then elected, shall continue in office until the first general election under this Constitution.

Eighth. The first general election under this Constitution shall be held in the year one thousand eight hundred and fifty-two.

Ninth The first election for Governor, Lieutenant Governor, Judges of the Supreme Court and Circuit Courts, Clerk of the Supreme Court, Prosecuting Attorney, Secretary, Auditor, and Treasurer of State, and State Superintendent of Public Instruction, under this Constitution, shall be held at the general election in the year one thousand eight hundred and fifty-two; and such of said officers as may be in office when this Constitution shall go into effect, shall continue in their respective offices until their successors shall have been elected and qualified.

Tenth. Every person elected by popular vote, and now in any office which is continued by this Constitution, and every person who shall be so elected to any such office before the taking effect of this Constitution (except as in this Constitution otherwise provided), shall continue in office until the term for which such person has been, or may be, elected, shall expire · *Provided,* That no such person shall continue in office after the taking effect of this Constitution, for a longer period than the term of such office in this Constitution prescribed

Eleventh. On the taking effect of this Constitution, all officers thereby continued in office shall, before proceeding in the further discharge of their duties, take an oath or affirmation to support this Constitution.

Twelfth. All vacancies that may occur in existing offices prior to the first general election under this Constitution, shall be filled in the manner now prescribed by law.

Thirteenth. At the time of submitting this Constitution to the electors for their approval or disapproval, the article numbered thirteen, in relation to negroes and mulattoes, shall be submitted as a distinct proposition, in the following form : "Exclusion and Colonization of Negroes and Mulattoes," "Aye," or

"No." And if a majority of the votes cast shall be in favor of said article, then the same shall form a part of this Constitution, otherwise it shall be void and form no part thereof.

Fourteenth. No article or section of this Constitution shall be submitted as a distinct proposition to a vote of the electors otherwise than as herein provided.

Fifteenth. Whenever a portion of the citizens of the counties of Perry and Spencer shall deem it expedient to form, of the contiguous territory of said counties, a new county, it shall be the duty of those interested in the organization of such new county, to lay off the same by proper metes and bounds of equal portions as nearly as practicable, not to exceed one-third of the territory of each of said counties. The proposal to create such new county shall be submitted to the voters of said counties, at a general election, in such manner as shall be prescribed by law. And if a majority of all the votes given at said election shall be in favor of the organization of said new county, it shall be the duty of the General Assembly to organize the same out of the territory thus designated.

Sixteenth. The General Assembly may alter or amend the charter of Clarksville, and make such regulations as may be necessary for carrying into effect the objects contemplated in granting the same, and the funds belonging to said town shall be applied according to the intention of the grantor.

Done in Convention, at Indianapolis, the tenth day of February, in the year of our Lord, one thousand eight hundred and fifty-one; and of the independence of the United States, the seventy-fifth.

GEORGE WHITFIELD CARR,
President and Delegate from the County of Lawrence.

Attest: WM. H. ENGLISH,
      Principal Secretary.

GEO. L. SITES,
HERMAN G. BARKWELL,
ROBERT M. EVANS,
      Assistant Secretaries.

CPSIA information can be obtained
at www.ICGtesting.com
Printed in the USA
BVHW040839230720
584407BV00006B/136